Easy -to- Bake

RECIPES

Publications International, Ltd.

Microwave Cooking: Microwave ovens vary in wattage. Use the cooking times as guidelines and check for doneness before adding more time.

Preparation/Cooking Times: Preparation times are based on the approximate amount of time required to assemble the recipe before cooking, baking, chilling or serving. These times include preparation steps such as measuring, chopping and mixing. The fact that some preparations and cooking can be done simultaneously is taken into account. Preparation of optional ingredients and serving suggestions is not included.

table of
contents

speedycookies

Orange Pecan Cookies

Makes about 3 dozen cookies

> 1 package (about 17 ounces) sugar cookie mix
> ½ cup butter, melted
> 1 egg, slightly beaten
> 1 teaspoon grated orange peel
> ½ cup chopped pecans
> ½ cup powdered sugar
> 1½ teaspoons orange juice

Preheat oven to 375°F.

Combine cookie mix, butter, egg and orange peel in large bowl. Stir with spoon until well blended. Stir in pecans.

Drop dough by rounded teaspoonfuls onto *ungreased* cookie sheets about 2 inches apart. Bake for 7 to 8 minutes or until set. Cool 1 minute on cookie sheets. Remove to wire racks; cool completely.

Combine powdered sugar and orange juice in small bowl; stir until well blended. Drizzle over top of cooled cookies. Allow glaze to set before storing between layers of waxed paper in airtight container.

Chips Ahoy!® Wiches

Makes 12 sandwich cookies

> 24 CHIPS AHOY!® Chocolate Chip Cookies
> 3 cups any flavor ice cream, sherbet, frozen yogurt or whipped topping
> Sprinkles, chocolate chips, chopped nuts, toasted or tinted coconut, or other assorted small candies

1. Spread ¼ cup ice cream on flat side of each of 12 cookies. Place remaining cookies on top. Roll or lightly press edges in sprinkles.

2. Freeze until firm, about 4 hours.

Peanut Butter Chipwiches: Spread about 1 tablespoon peanut butter on flat side of each of 12 cookies; top with a banana slice. Continue as directed above.

Orange Pecan Cookies

speedycookies

Flourless Peanut Butter Cookies

Makes about 2 dozen cookies

> **1 cup peanut butter**
> **1 cup packed light brown sugar**
> **1 egg**
> **24 milk chocolate candy stars or other solid milk chocolate candy**

Preheat oven to 350°F. Combine peanut butter, sugar and egg in medium bowl; beat until blended and smooth.

Shape dough into 24 balls about 1½ inches in diameter. Place 2 inches apart on ungreased cookie sheets. Press one chocolate star on top of each cookie. Bake 10 to 12 minutes or until set. Transfer to wire racks to cool completely.

Coconut Clouds

Makes 3½ dozen cookies

> **2⅔ cups flaked coconut, divided**
> **1 package DUNCAN HINES® Moist Deluxe® Classic Yellow Cake Mix**
> **1 egg**
> **½ cup vegetable oil**
> **¼ cup water**
> **1 teaspoon almond extract**

1. Preheat oven to 350°F. Reserve 1⅓ cups coconut in medium bowl.

2. Combine cake mix, egg, oil, water and almond extract in large bowl. Beat at low speed with electric mixer. Stir in remaining 1⅓ cups coconut. Drop rounded teaspoonful dough into reserved coconut. Roll to cover lightly. Place on ungreased baking sheet. Repeat with remaining dough, placing balls 2 inches apart. Bake at 350°F 10 to 12 minutes or until light golden brown. Cool 1 minute on baking sheets. Remove to cooling racks. Cool completely. Store in airtight container.

Cook's Note: To save time when forming dough into balls, use a 1-inch spring-operated cookie scoop. Spring-operated cookie scoops are available at kitchen specialty shops.

Flourless Peanut Butter Cookies

speedycookies

Easy Lemon Cookies

Makes 4 dozen cookies

> **1 package DUNCAN HINES® Moist Deluxe® Lemon Cake Mix**
> **2 eggs**
> **½ cup vegetable oil**
> **1 teaspoon grated lemon peel**
> **Pecan halves, for garnish**

1. Preheat oven to 350°F.

2. Combine cake mix, eggs, oil and lemon peel in large bowl. Stir until thoroughly blended. Drop by rounded teaspoonfuls 2 inches apart onto ungreased cookie sheets. Press pecan half in center of each cookie. Bake at 350°F for 9 to 11 minutes or until edges are light golden brown. Cool 1 minute on cookie sheets. Remove to wire racks. Cool completely. Store in airtight container.

Tip: You may substitute whole almonds or walnut halves for the pecan halves.

Chocolate Chip 'n Oatmeal Cookies

Makes about 4 dozen cookies

> **1 package (18.25 or 18.5 ounces) yellow cake mix**
> **1 cup quick-cooking rolled oats, uncooked**
> **¾ cup butter or margarine, softened**
> **2 eggs**
> **1 cup HERSHEY₀S Semi-Sweet Chocolate Chips**

Heat oven to 350°F.

Combine cake mix, oats, butter and eggs in large bowl; mix well. Stir in chocolate chips. Drop by rounded teaspoons onto ungreased cookie sheets.

Bake 10 to 12 minutes or until very lightly browned. Cool slightly; remove from cookie sheets to wire racks. Cool completely.

Easy Lemon Cookies

Chocolate Peanut Butter Chip Cookies

Makes about 4 dozen cookies

Prep Time: 15 minutes
Bake Time: 6 to 8 minutes

> 8 (1-ounce) squares semi-sweet chocolate
> 3 tablespoons butter or margarine
> 1 (14-ounce) can **EAGLE® BRAND** Sweetened Condensed Milk (**NOT** evaporated milk)
> 2 cups biscuit baking mix
> 1 egg
> 1 teaspoon vanilla extract
> 1 cup (6 ounces) peanut butter-flavored chips

1. Preheat oven to 350°F. In large saucepan, over low heat, melt chocolate and butter with Eagle Brand; remove from heat. Add biscuit mix, egg and vanilla; with mixer, beat until smooth and well blended.

2. Let mixture cool to room temperature. Stir in peanut butter chips. Shape into 1¼-inch balls. Place 2 inches apart on ungreased baking sheets. Bake 6 to 8 minutes or until tops are slightly crusty. Cool. Store tightly covered at room temperature.

Chocolate Macadamia Chippers

Makes 2 dozen cookies

> 1 package (18 ounces) refrigerated chocolate chip cookie dough
> 3 tablespoons unsweetened cocoa powder
> ½ cup coarsely chopped macadamia nuts

Preheat oven to 375°F. Remove dough from wrapper according to package directions.

Place dough in medium bowl; stir in cocoa until well blended. (Dough may be kneaded lightly, if desired.) Stir in nuts. Drop by heaping tablespoons 2 inches apart onto ungreased cookie sheets.

Bake 9 to 11 minutes or until almost set. Transfer to wire racks to cool completely.

Chocolate Peanut Butter Chip Cookies

Peanut Butter Surprise Cookies

Makes about 4 dozen cookies

24 miniature peanut butter cups
1 can (14 ounces) sweetened condensed milk (not evaporated milk)
¾ cup creamy peanut butter
¼ Butter Flavor CRISCO® Stick or ¼ cup Butter Flavor CRISCO® all-vegetable shortening
1 egg
1 teaspoon vanilla
2 cups regular all-purpose baking mix

1. Remove wrappers from peanut butter cups. Cut candy into quarters.

2. Combine condensed milk, peanut butter, ¼ cup shortening, egg and vanilla in large bowl. Beat at medium speed of electric mixer until smooth. Add baking mix. Beat until well blended. Stir in candy pieces with spoon. Cover. Refrigerate 1 hour.

3. Heat oven to 350°F. Place sheets of foil on countertop for cooling cookies.

4. Drop dough by slightly rounded teaspoonfuls 2 inches apart onto ungreased baking sheet. Shape into balls with spoon.

5. Bake at 350°F for 7 to 9 minutes or until light brown around edges and center is just set. *Do not overbake.* Cool 2 minutes on baking sheet. Remove cookies to foil to cool completely.

Variation: Shape dough into 1¼-inch balls. Place 2 inches apart onto ungreased baking sheet. Dip fork in flour; flatten dough slightly in crisscross pattern.

Peanut Butter Surprise Cookies

express bars

Chocolate Nut Bars

Makes 24 to 36 bars

Prep Time: 10 minutes
Bake Time: 33 to 38 minutes

> 1¾ cups graham cracker crumbs
> ½ cup (1 stick) butter or margarine, melted
> 1 (14-ounce) can EAGLE® BRAND Sweetened Condensed Milk (NOT evaporated milk)
> 2 cups (12 ounces) semi-sweet chocolate chips, divided
> 1 teaspoon vanilla extract
> 1 cup chopped nuts

1. Preheat oven to 375°F. Combine crumbs and butter; press firmly on bottom of 13×9-inch baking pan. Bake 8 minutes. *Reduce oven temperature to 350°F.*

2. In small saucepan, melt Eagle Brand with 1 cup chocolate chips and vanilla. Spread chocolate mixture over prepared crust. Top with remaining 1 cup chocolate chips, then nuts; press down firmly.

3. Bake 25 to 30 minutes. Cool. Chill if desired. Cut into bars. Store loosely covered at room temperature.

Coconut Raspberry Bars

Sweetheart Layer Bars

Makes about 36 bars

1 cup (2 sticks) butter or margarine, divided
1½ cups finely crushed unsalted thin pretzels or pretzel sticks
1 cup HERSHEY'S MINI KISSES™ Milk Chocolates or Semi-Sweet Chocolates
1 can (14 ounces) sweetened condensed milk (not evaporated milk)
¾ cup HERSHEY'S Cocoa
2 cups MOUNDS® Sweetened Coconut Flakes, tinted*

*To tint coconut: Place 1 teaspoon water and ½ teaspoon red food color in small bowl; stir in 2 cups coconut flakes. With fork, toss until evenly coated.

Heat oven to 350°F.

Put ¾ cup butter in 13×9×2-inch baking pan; place in oven just until butter melts. Remove from oven. Stir in crushed pretzels; press evenly into bottom of pan. Sprinkle Mini Kisses™ over pretzel layer.

Place sweetened condensed milk, cocoa and remaining ¼ cup butter in small microwave-safe bowl. Microwave at HIGH (100%) 1 to 1½ minutes or until mixture is melted and smooth when stirred; carefully pour over pretzel layer in pan. Top with coconut; press firmly down onto chocolate layer.

Bake 25 to 30 minutes or until lightly browned around edges. Cool completely in pan on wire rack. Cut into heart-shaped pieces with cookie cutters or cut into bars.

Sweetheart Layer Bars

easy cheesecakes

Chocolate Raspberry Cheesecake

Makes 8 servings

Prep Time: 15 minutes
Chill Time: 3 hours

>   2 (3-ounce) packages cream cheese, softened
>   1 (14-ounce) can sweetened condensed milk
>   1 egg
>   3 tablespoons lemon juice
>   1 teaspoon vanilla
>   1 cup fresh or frozen raspberries
>   1 (6-ounce) READY CRUST® Chocolate Pie Crust
>   Chocolate Glaze (recipe follows)

Preheat oven to 350°F. Beat cream cheese in medium bowl with electric mixer at medium speed until fluffy. Gradually beat in sweetened condensed milk until smooth. Add egg, lemon juice and vanilla; mix well. Arrange raspberries on bottom of crust. Slowly pour cream cheese mixture over raspberries.

Bake 30 to 35 minutes or until center is almost set. Cool on wire rack.

Prepare Chocolate Glaze; spread over cheesecake. Refrigerate 3 hours. Garnish as desired. Refrigerate leftovers.

Chocolate Glaze: Melt 2 (1-ounce) squares semisweet baking chocolate with ¼ cup whipping cream in small saucepan over low heat. Cook and stir until thickened and smooth. Remove from heat.

Chocolate Raspberry Cheesecake

Philadelphia® 3-Step® Mini Cheesecakes

Makes 12 servings

Prep Time: 10 minutes
Bake Time: 20 minutes

> **2 packages (8 ounces each) PHILADELPHIA® Cream Cheese, softened**
> **½ cup sugar**
> **½ teaspoon vanilla**
> **2 eggs**
> **12 NILLA® Wafer**
> **Fresh fruit**

BEAT cream cheese, sugar and vanilla with electric mixer on medium speed until well blended. Add eggs, 1 at a time, mixing on low speed after each addition just until blended.

PLACE 1 wafer on bottom of each of 12 paper-lined muffin cups. Pour batter evenly into prepared cups.

BAKE at 350°F for 20 minutes or until centers are almost set. Cool. Refrigerate 3 hours or overnight. Top with fresh fruit just before serving.

Great Substitute: Substitute OREO® Chocolate Sandwich Cookies for NILLA® Wafers.

Cheesecake Squares: Omit wafers. Line 8-inch square baking pan with foil. Mix 1½ cups HONEY MAID® Graham Cracker Crumbs or OREO® Chocolate Cookie Crumbs with ¼ cup butter (½ stick), melted; press onto bottom of prepared pan. Prepare cheesecake batter as directed. Pour over crust. Bake and cool as directed. Cut into squares.

Philadelphia® 3-Step Mini Cheesecakes

Sweetheart Cheesecake

Makes 10 servings

> **1¼ cups chocolate cookie crumbs**
> **¼ cup butter, melted**
> **2 packages (8 ounces each) cream cheese, softened**
> **½ cup plus 1 tablespoon sugar, divided**
> **1 teaspoon vanilla, divided**
> **2 eggs**
> **1 cup sour cream**
> **1 can (21 ounces) cherry pie filling**

Preheat oven to 350°F.

For crust, combine cookie crumbs and butter until well blended. Press mixture onto bottom of 9-inch springform pan. Bake 8 minutes; cool.

For filling, beat cream cheese, ½ cup sugar and ½ teaspoon vanilla in medium bowl with electric mixer until well blended. Beat in eggs. Pour into cooled crust; bake about 40 minutes or until center is almost set. Cool.

For topping, combine sour cream, remaining 1 teaspoon sugar and remaining ½ teaspoon vanilla in small bowl. Spread evenly over top of cheesecake. Drop teaspoonfuls of sauce from cherry pie filling onto sour cream topping; carefully pull tip of knife or wooden skewer through cherry sauce to form hearts. Cover and refrigerate 3 hours or overnight. Serve remaining cherry pie filling over slices of cheesecake.

Sweetheart Cheesecake

Philadelphia® 3-STEP®
Caramel Pecan Cheesecake

Makes 8 servings

Prep Time: 10 minutes
Bake Time: 40 minutes

- **2 packages (8 ounces each) PHILADELPHIA® Cream Cheese, softened**
- **½ cup sugar**
- **½ teaspoon vanilla**
- **2 eggs**
- **20 KRAFT® Caramels**
- **2 tablespoons milk**
- **½ cup chopped PLANTERS® Pecans**
- **1 HONEY MAID® Graham Pie Crust (6 ounces)**

MIX cream cheese, sugar and vanilla with electric mixer on medium speed until well blended. Add eggs; mix until blended. Melt caramels with milk on low heat, stirring frequently until smooth. Stir in pecans.

POUR caramel mixture into crust. Pour cream cheese batter over caramel mixture.

BAKE at 350°F for 40 minutes or until center is almost set. Cool. Refrigerate 3 hours or overnight. Garnish as desired.

How To Easily Slice Cheesecake: Let cheesecake stand at room temperature for at least 30 minutes before slicing to allow caramel layer to soften.

Philadelphia® 3-Step® Caramel Pecan Cheesecake

quick
cakes

Easy Cappuccino Cake

Makes 14 servings

Prep Time: 25 minutes

> 1 package (2-layer size) white cake mix
> 4 tablespoons MAXWELL HOUSE® Instant Coffee, divided
> ¼ cup milk plus 1 tablespoon milk
> 4 squares BAKER'S® Semi-Sweet Baking Chocolate, melted
> 2 tubs (8 ounces each) COOL WHIP® Whipped Topping, thawed, divided

HEAT oven to 350°F.

PREPARE and bake cake mix as directed on package for 8- or 9-inch round pans, adding 2 tablespoons instant coffee to cake mix.

POUR ¼ cup milk and 1 tablespoon instant coffee into small bowl, stirring until coffee is dissolved. Slowly stir into melted chocolate until smooth. Cool completely. Gently stir in 1 tub of whipped topping. Refrigerate 20 minutes or until well chilled.

MEANWHILE, mix 1 tablespoon milk and 1 tablespoon coffee until dissolved. Gently stir into remaining tub of whipped topping.

COVER one cake layer with chocolate mixture. Place second cake layer on top. Frost top and side of cake with coffee-flavored whipped topping. Refrigerate until ready to serve.

Variation: If desired, omit the coffee for a delicious plain chocolate filled layer cake.

Easy Cappuccino Cake

Luscious Lemon Poke Cake

Makes 12 servings

Preparation Time: 30 minutes
Refrigerating Time: 4 hours

> **2 baked 8- or 9-inch round white cake layers, cooled completely**
> **2 cups boiling water**
> **1 package (8-serving size) *or* 2 packages (4-serving size) JELL-O® Brand Lemon Flavor Gelatin Dessert**
> **1 tub (8 or 12 ounces) COOL WHIP® Whipped Topping, thawed**

PLACE cake layers, top sides up, in 2 clean 8- or 9-inch round cake pans. Pierce cake with large fork at ½-inch intervals.

STIR boiling water into gelatin in medium bowl at least 2 minutes until completely dissolved. Carefully pour 1 cup of the gelatin over 1 cake layer. Pour remaining gelatin over second cake layer. Refrigerate 3 hours.

DIP 1 cake pan in warm water 10 seconds; unmold onto serving plate. Spread with about 1 cup of the whipped topping. Unmold second cake layer; carefully place on first cake layer. Frost top and side of cake with remaining whipped topping.

REFRIGERATE at least 1 hour or until ready to serve. Decorate as desired.

Luscious Lemon Poke Cake

quickcakes

Easy Egg Nog Pound Cake

Makes 1 (10-inch) cake

Prep Time: 10 minutes
Bake Time: 40 to 45 minutes

> 1 (18.25-ounce) package yellow cake mix
> 1 (4-serving-size) package instant vanilla pudding and pie filling mix
> ¾ cup **BORDEN®** Egg Nog
> ¾ cup vegetable oil
> 4 eggs
> ½ teaspoon ground nutmeg
> Powdered sugar, if desired

1. Preheat oven to 350°F.

2. In large mixing bowl, combine cake mix, pudding mix, Borden Egg Nog and oil; beat at low speed until moistened. Add eggs and nutmeg; beat at medium-high speed 4 minutes.

3. Pour into greased and floured 10-inch fluted or tube pan.

4. Bake 40 to 45 minutes or until toothpick inserted near center comes out clean.

5. Cool 10 minutes; remove from pan. Cool completely. Sprinkle with powdered sugar, if desired.

Easy Egg Nog Pound Cake

Kahlúa® Black Forest Cake

Makes 1 (9-inch) cake

   **1 package (18¼ ounces) chocolate fudge cake mix with
      pudding**
   3 eggs
   ¾ cup water
   ½ cup KAHLÚA® Liqueur
   ⅓ cup vegetable oil
   1 can (16 ounces) vanilla or chocolate frosting
   1 can (21 ounces) cherry filling and topping
      **Chocolate sprinkles or chocolate shavings for garnish
      (optional)**

Preheat oven to 350°F. Grease and flour 2 (9-inch) cake pans; set
aside. In large mixer bowl, prepare cake mix according to package
directions, using eggs, water, Kahlúa® and oil. Pour batter into
prepared pans. Bake 25 to 35 minutes or until toothpick inserted in
center comes out clean. Cool cake in pans 10 minutes; turn layers out
onto wire racks to cool completely.

Place one cake layer bottom side up on serving plate. Spread thick
layer of frosting in circle, 1½ inches around outer edge of cake. Spoon
half of cherry filling into center of cake layer to frosting edge. Top with
second cake layer, bottom side down. Repeat with frosting and
remaining cherry filling. Spread remaining frosting around side of cake.
Decorate with chocolate sprinkles or shavings, if desired.

Kahlúa® Black Forest Cake

effortless
pies

Apple-Raisin Cobbler Pie

Makes 8 servings

Prep Time: 10 minutes
Baking Time: 35 minutes

    2 (20-ounce) cans apple pie filling
    1 cup raisins
    ¼ teaspoon ground nutmeg
    1 (6-ounce) READY CRUST® Shortbread Pie Crust
    ⅓ cup all-purpose flour
    ¼ cup packed brown sugar
    3 tablespoons butter or margarine, melted
    ¾ cup chopped walnuts

Preheat oven to 375°F.

Combine pie filling, raisins and nutmeg in large bowl. Spoon into crust.
Combine flour and sugar in small bowl; stir in butter until crumbly. Stir
in walnuts; sprinkle over filling.

Bake 35 to 45 minutes or until topping is golden.

Apple-Raisin Cobbler Pie

Confetti Pie

Makes 8 servings

Prep Time: 15 minutes plus refrigerating

> **1 boiling water**
> **1 package (4-serving size) JELL-O® Brand Lemon Flavor Gelatin**
> **½ cup cold water**
> **1 cup boiling water**
> **1 package (4-serving size) JELL-O® Brand Orange Flavor Gelatin**
> **½ cup cold orange juice**
> **2 cups thawed COOL WHIP® Whipped Topping**
> **⅓ cup multi-colored sprinkles**
> **1 HONEY MAID® Honey Graham Pie Crust (9 inch)**

STIR 1 cup boiling water into lemon gelatin in medium bowl at least 2 minutes until completely dissolved. Stir in cold water. Pour into 8-inch square pan. Refrigerate 4 hours or until firm. Cut into ½-inch cubes.

STIR 1 cup boiling water into orange gelatin in large bowl at least 2 minutes until completely dissolved. Stir in orange juice. Refrigerate about 20 minutes or until slightly thickened (consistency of unbeaten egg whites). Gently stir in whipped topping. Gently stir in gelatin cubes and sprinkles. Refrigerate until mixture will mound. Pour into crust.

REFRIGERATE at least 4 hours or until firm. Garnish with additional whipped topping and sprinkles, if desired.

Great Substitutes: Try Berry Blue or Lime Flavor Gelatin instead of Lemon Flavor when making the gelatin cubes.

Confetti Pie

effortless**pies**

Pumpkin Pie Crunch
Makes 16 to 20 servings

> **1 can (16 ounces) solid pack pumpkin**
> **1 can (12 ounces) evaporated milk**
> **3 eggs**
> **1½ cups sugar**
> **4 teaspoons pumpkin pie spice**
> **½ teaspoon salt**
> **1 package DUNCAN HINES® Moist Deluxe® Classic Yellow Cake Mix**
> **1 cup chopped pecans**
> **1 cup butter or margarine, melted**
> **Whipped topping**

1. Preheat oven to 350°F. Grease bottom of 13×9×2-inch pan.

2. Combine pumpkin, evaporated milk, eggs, sugar, pumpkin pie spice and salt in large bowl. Pour into pan. Sprinkle dry cake mix evenly over pumpkin mixture. Top with pecans. Drizzle with melted butter. Bake at 350°F 50 to 55 minutes or until golden. Cool completely. Serve with whipped topping. Refrigerate leftovers.

Tip: For a richer flavor, try using Duncan Hines® Moist Deluxe® Butter Recipe Golden Cake Mix.

Pumpkin Pie Crunch

effortlesspies

Orange Pecan Pie

Makes 8 servings

> 3 eggs
> ½ cup GRANDMA'S® Molasses
> ½ cup light corn syrup
> ¼ cup orange juice
> 1 teaspoon grated orange peel
> 1 teaspoon vanilla
> 1½ cups whole pecan halves
> 1 (9-inch) unbaked pie shell
> Whipping cream (optional)

Heat oven to 350°F. In large bowl, beat eggs. Add molasses, corn syrup, orange juice, orange peel and vanilla; beat until well blended. Stir in pecans. Pour into unbaked pie shell. Bake 30 to 45 minutes or until filling sets. Cool on wire rack. Serve with whipping cream, if desired.

No Bake Peanut Butter Pie

Makes 1 pie

> 4 ounces cream cheese
> 1 cup confectioners' sugar, sifted
> 1 cup crunchy peanut butter
> ½ cup milk
> 8 ounces frozen whipped topping, thawed
> 1 deep-dish graham cracker or chocolate-flavored crust

In large mixer bowl combine cream cheese and confectioners' sugar; mix well. Add peanut butter and mix. Slowly add milk and mix well. Fold in whipped topping. Pour into pie shell and cover. Freeze for at least 30 minutes. If desired, drizzle each serving with chocolate syrup.

Favorite recipe from *Peanut Advisory Board*

Orange Pecan Pie

simple breads

Pumpkin Bread

Makes 2 loaves

- 1 package (about 18 ounces) yellow cake mix
- 1 can (16 ounces) solid pack pumpkin
- ⅓ cup GRANDMA'S® Molasses
- 4 eggs
- 1 teaspoon cinnamon
- 1 teaspoon nutmeg
- ⅓ cup nuts, chopped (optional)
- ⅓ cup raisins (optional)

Preheat oven to 350°F. Grease two 9×5-inch loaf pans.

Combine all ingredients in a large bowl and mix well. Beat at medium speed 2 minutes. Pour into prepared pans. Bake 60 minutes or until toothpick inserted into center comes out clean.

Hint: Serve with cream cheese or preserves, or top with cream cheese frosting or ice cream.

Pumpkin Bread

Gooey Caramel and Chocolate Pecan Rolls

Makes 24 rolls

> **2 loaves (1 pound each) frozen white bread dough**
> **1 jar (12 ounces) caramel ice cream topping**
> **⅔ cup coarsely chopped pecans**
> **1 cup semisweet chocolate chips, divided**
> **4 tablespoons butter, divided**

1. Thaw bread dough according to package directions.

2. Preheat oven to 375°F. Divide caramel topping evenly between two 9-inch round cake pans; spread in thin layer. Sprinkle pecans evenly over caramel.

3. Microwave ⅔ cup chocolate chips and 2 tablespoons butter in medium microwavable bowl on HIGH (100% power) for 30 seconds; stir. Microwave for 20 second intervals, if necessary, stirring until smooth; set aside.

4. On lightly floured surface, roll one loaf bread dough into 12×8-inch rectangle. Spread half chocolate mixture over dough. Beginning from the long side, roll up jelly-roll style to form 12-inch log, pinching seam to seal. Slice into 12 rolls; arrange cut side down in 1 prepared pan. Repeat with remaining dough and chocolate mixture.

5. Cover; let rise in warm place until nearly doubled, about 1 hour. Uncover; bake 20 to 25 minutes. Immediately invert onto serving plates.

6. Melt remaining ⅓ cup chocolate chips and 2 tablespoons butter in microwave as directed in step 3. Drizzle over warm rolls.

Gooey Caramel and Chocolate Pecan Rolls

Streusel Coffeecake

Makes 24 servings

Preparation Time: 25 minutes
Cook Time: 40 minutes
Cooling Time: 2 hours
Total Time: 3 hours and 5 minutes

32 CHIPS AHOY!® Chocolate Chip Cookies, divided
1 (18- to 18½-ounce) package yellow or white cake mix
½ cup BREAKSTONE'S® or KNUDSEN® Sour Cream
½ cup PLANTERS® Pecans, chopped
½ cup BAKER'S® ANGEL FLAKE® Coconut
¼ cup packed brown sugar
1 teaspoon ground cinnamon
⅓ cup margarine or butter, melted
Powdered sugar glaze (optional)

1. Coarsely chop 20 cookies; finely crush remaining 12 cookies. Set aside.

2. Prepare cake mix batter according to package directions; blend in sour cream. Stir in chopped cookies. Pour batter into greased and floured 13×9×2-inch baking pan.

3. Mix cookie crumbs, pecans, coconut, brown sugar and cinnamon; stir in margarine or butter. Sprinkle over cake batter.

4. Bake at 350°F for 40 minutes or until toothpick inserted in center of cake comes out clean. Cool completely. Drizzle with powdered sugar glaze if desired. Cut into squares to serve.

Streusel Coffeecake

Cinnamon Chip Filled Crescents

Makes 16 crescents

> **2 cans (8 ounces each) refrigerated quick crescent dinner rolls**
> **2 tablespoons butter or margarine, melted**
> **1⅔ cups (10-ounce package) HERSHEY®S Cinnamon Chips, divided**
> **Cinnamon Chips Drizzle (recipe follows)**

Heat oven to 375°F. Unroll dough; separate into 16 triangles.

Spread melted butter on each triangle. Sprinkle 1 cup cinnamon chips evenly over triangles; gently press chips into dough. Roll from shortest side of triangle to opposite point. Place, point side down, on ungreased cookie sheet; curve into crescent shape.

Bake 8 to 10 minutes or until golden brown. Drizzle with Cinnamon Drizzle. Serve warm.

Cinnamon Chips Drizzle: Place remaining ⅔ cup chips and 1½ teaspoons shortening (do not use butter, margarine, spread or oil) in small microwave-safe bowl. Microwave at HIGH (100%) 1 minute; stir until chips are melted.

Cinnamon Chip Filled Crescents

Fast Pesto Focaccia

Makes 16 squares

Prep and Cook Time: 20 minutes

> **1 can (10 ounces) pizza crust dough**
> **2 tablespoons prepared pesto**
> **4 sun-dried tomatoes packed in oil, drained**

Preheat oven to 425°F. Lightly grease 8×8×2-inch pan. Unroll pizza dough; fold in half and pat into pan.

Spread pesto evenly over dough. Chop tomatoes or snip with kitchen scissors; sprinkle over pesto. Press tomatoes into dough. Make indentations in dough every 2 inches using wooden spoon handle.

Bake 10 to 12 minutes or until golden brown. Cut into squares and serve warm or at room temperature.

Quick Corn Bread with Chilies 'n' Cheese

Makes 16 servings

> **1 package (12 to 16 ounces) corn bread or corn muffin mix**
> **1 cup (4 ounces) shredded Monterey Jack cheese, divided**
> **1 can (4 ounces) chopped green chilies, drained**
> **1 envelope LIPTON® RECIPE SECRETS® Vegetable Soup Mix**

Prepare corn bread mix according to package directions; stir in ½ cup cheese, chilies and vegetable soup mix. Pour batter into lightly greased 8-inch baking pan; bake as directed. While warm, top with remaining ½ cup cheese. Cool completely on wire rack. To serve, cut into squares.

Fast Pesto Focaccia

acknowledgments

The publisher would like to thank the companies and organizations listed below for the use of their recipes and photographs in this publication.

CHIPS AHOY!® Chocolate Chip Cookies

Duncan Hines® and Moist Deluxe® are registered trademarks of Aurora Foods Inc.

Eagle® Brand

Grandma's® is a registered trademark of Mott's, Inc.

Hershey Foods Corporation

Kahlúa® Liqueur

Keebler® Company

Kraft Foods Holdings

© Mars, Incorporated 2002

Peanut Advisory Board

The Quaker® Oatmeal Kitchens

© 2002 The J.M. Smucker Co. All rights reserved

Unilever Bestfoods North America

index

METRIC CONVERSION CHART

VOLUME MEASUREMENTS (dry)

$\frac{1}{8}$ teaspoon = 0.5 mL
$\frac{1}{4}$ teaspoon = 1 mL
$\frac{1}{2}$ teaspoon = 2 mL
$\frac{3}{4}$ teaspoon = 4 mL
1 teaspoon = 5 mL
1 tablespoon = 15 mL
2 tablespoons = 30 mL
$\frac{1}{4}$ cup = 60 mL
$\frac{1}{3}$ cup = 75 mL
$\frac{1}{2}$ cup = 125 mL
$\frac{2}{3}$ cup = 150 mL
$\frac{3}{4}$ cup = 175 mL
1 cup = 250 mL
2 cups = 1 pint = 500 mL
3 cups = 750 mL
4 cups = 1 quart = 1 L

VOLUME MEASUREMENTS (fluid)

1 fluid ounce (2 tablespoons) = 30 mL
4 fluid ounces ($\frac{1}{2}$ cup) = 125 mL
8 fluid ounces (1 cup) = 250 mL
12 fluid ounces ($1\frac{1}{2}$ cups) = 375 mL
16 fluid ounces (2 cups) = 500 mL

WEIGHTS (mass)

$\frac{1}{2}$ ounce = 15 g
1 ounce = 30 g
3 ounces = 90 g
4 ounces = 120 g
8 ounces = 225 g
10 ounces = 285 g
12 ounces = 360 g
16 ounces = 1 pound = 450 g

DIMENSIONS

$\frac{1}{16}$ inch = 2 mm
$\frac{1}{8}$ inch = 3 mm
$\frac{1}{4}$ inch = 6 mm
$\frac{1}{2}$ inch = 1.5 cm
$\frac{3}{4}$ inch = 2 cm
1 inch = 2.5 cm

OVEN TEMPERATURES

250°F = 120°C
275°F = 140°C
300°F = 150°C
325°F = 160°C
350°F = 180°C
375°F = 190°C
400°F = 200°C
425°F = 220°C
450°F = 230°C

BAKING PAN SIZES

Utensil	Size in Inches/Quarts	Metric Volume	Size in Centimeters
Baking or	8×8×2	2 L	20×20×5
Cake Pan	9×9×2	2.5 L	23×23×5
(square or	12×8×2	3 L	30×20×5
rectangular)	13×9×2	3.5 L	33×23×5
Loaf Pan	8×4×3	1.5 L	20×10×7
	9×5×3	2 L	23×13×7
Round Layer	8×1½	1.2 L	20×4
Cake Pan	9×1½	1.5 L	23×4
Pie Plate	8×1¼	750 mL	20×3
	9×1¼	1 L	23×3
Baking Dish	1 quart	1 L	—
or Casserole	1½ quart	1.5 L	—
	2 quart	2 L	—